Prince William County Virginia

Bond Book

August 1753-1782

Abstracted by
June Whitehurst Johnson

HERITAGE BOOKS
2011

HERITAGE BOOKS
AN IMPRINT OF HERITAGE BOOKS, INC.

Books, CDs, and more—Worldwide

For our listing of thousands of titles see our website
at
www.HeritageBooks.com

Published 2011 by
HERITAGE BOOKS, INC.
Publishing Division
100 Railroad Ave. #104
Westminster, Maryland 21157

Copyright © 1982 June Whitehurst Johnson

Other books by the author:

Prince William County, Virginia Bond Book: August 1753–1782

Prince William County, Virginia Deed Book: Liber D, 1738–1740

Prince William County, Virginia Will Book: Liber G, 1778–1791 and Order Book, 1769–1771

Prince William County, Virginia Will Book: Liber H, 1792–1803

Surviving Cameron Parish Records, Loudoun County, Virginia: Tithable List of 1765

All rights reserved. No part of this book may be reproduced or transmitted in any form or by any means, electronic or mechanical, including photocopying, recording or by any information storage and retrieval system without written permission from the author, except for the inclusion of brief quotations in a review.

International Standard Book Numbers
Paperbound: 978-1-58549-520-7
Clothbound: 978-0-7884-8797-2

PREFACE

The Administrator Bonds which follow were recently returned to the Virginia State Archives. There are about 169 bonds of which in comparing these to references to will probated and administration granted and previously know bonds both published in the County Note-book, there are about 135 new estates. This bond book also covers a period of time when there are will books missing for the county.

The first name in each bond is the decease, second of the administrator, and the other names of the securities.

I have no attempt to correct spelling. The surname is indexed by the most commonly used spelling. You will notice in the index that the page number to the decease's name is in bold print.

Prince William County, Virginia
Bond Book
August 1753 - 1782

Strother Settle dec.
Mary Settle Adm.; George Brown, Martin Settle. Aug. 27, 1753.

Jacob Smith dec.
Hermon Batton and Catherine Batton Adm.;
John Garner, John Camper;
Oct. 22, 1753.

Thomas Drummon dec.
Aron Drummon Adm.; James Head, Thos. Williams. Nov. 26, 1753.

John Farrow dec.
John Summers and Elizabeth Summers Adm;
John Metcalf and William Thorn.
March 25, 1754.

William Champlin dec.
William Goon Adm.; Henry Poulson and Aron Champlin. March 25, 1754.

Thos. Ward dec.
William Rookard Adm.; John Diskin.
June 24, 1754

James Farguson dec.
George Brett Adm.; Richard Kenner.
June 24, 1754.

Bryan Chambling Jr.? dec.
Mason Bennitt Adm., John Chapman Purcell, John Farrow. June 24, 1754.

William Gallahue dec.
Ann Gallahue Adm.; Richard Kenner and George Calvert Jr., Nath. Overhall.
June 24, 1754.

Robt. Marshall dec.
Margaret Marshall Adm.
Simon Luttrell, Isaac Farrow, and William Rookard. June 24, 1754.

Robert Marshall dec.
Robert Marshall and Thomas Marshall Adm.; John Peyton Jr., John Simmons, and Scarlet Maddin. Sept. 24, 1754.

Margaret Marshall dec.;
Simon Lutterill Adm.; William Ashmore.
Sept. 24, 1754.

Henry Watkins dec.
Anne Watkins Adm.; John Addams and William Watkins. Nov. 26, 1754.

William Oakley dec.
Jemima Oakley Adm.; William Bridges and John Hopper. April 28, 1755.

Waller Seales dec.
Francis Jackson Adm.; Benjamin Bridges. Mary 26, 1755.

Thos. Scott dec.
Mary Scott Adm.; Richard Crupper and George Calvert. July 28, 1755.

Mary Hall dec.
Edward Hall Adm.; John Kelly, Henry Cooper. Aug. 26, 1755.

Robert Crupper dec.
John Baylis Adm.; Henry Lee. Aug. 26, 1755.

John Wright dec.
James Douglass, Allan McCrae, and John Graham. Sept. 23, 1755.

Wm. Russell dec.
William Russell Adm.; Parish Garner and John Conyers. March 22, 1756.

James Towers dec.
Mathew Steale Adm.; Foushee Tebbs.

March 22, 1756.

Thos. Mitchell dec.
Matthew Steele and Allan McCrae Adm.;
John Baylis and Thomas Macken.
May 24, 1756.

Humphry Pope dec.
Bertrand Ewell Adm.; Lynaugh Helm,
William Ashmore, Darby Gallahue, and
John Peyton. May 24, 1756.

John Carr dec.
William Carr Adm.; George Brett.
May 25, 1756.

James Belfare dec.
Sarah Belfare Adm.; Henry Churchill,
Gent. June 28, 1756.

Wm. Jones dec.
Solomon Jones Adm.; Charles Chinn and
James Young. Aug. 23, 1756.

Thomas Dallas dec.
Vylett Dallas Adm.; John Sias and
Thomas Davis. Oct. 25, 1756.

Thomas Stamps dec.
Ledia Stamps Adm.; Joseph Duncan and

John Duncan. Nov. 22, 1756.

William Green dec.
William Carr Adm.; William Ellzey.
Nov. 22, 1756.

William Spiller dec.
William Spiller Adm.; William Tackett and George Dodson. Feb. 28, 1757.

John Hamrick dec.
Sarah Hamrick Adm.; Richard Melton and Thomas Stone. Feb. 28, 1757.

David McCaul dec.
Allan McCrae Adm.; W. Ellzey, Bertrand Ewell. Feb. 28, 1757.

James Fearnsly dec.
Sarah Fearnsley Adm.; William Miller and Joseph Blackwell. March 28, 1757.

Thomas Doolittle dec.
Absolom Raimey Adm.; Francis Burgess and Joseph Kelly. March 28, 1757.

Robert Hamrick dec.
Elizabeth Hamrick Adm.; Samuel Stone

and John Smith.   May 23, 1757.

James Curtis dec.
Mathew Steele Adm.;   Thos. Macken?.   May 23, 1757.

Richd. Marshall dec.
Thomas Marshall Adm.;   Richard Crupper. May 24, 1757.

George Smith dec.
William Ellzey Adm.;   John Frogg.   Nov. 29, 1757.

John Anderson dec.
Elizabeth Anderson Adm.;   Thomas Bland and Richard Rixey.   March 27, 1758.

Francis Owen dec.
William Dawkins Adm.;   John Tyler and Robert Sinclair.   March 27, 1758.

John Wilson dec.
Jean Wilson Adm.;   Thomas James and Thomas Green.   March 27, 1758.

John Metcalf dec.
Dianah Metcalf Adm.;   William Hagard and

Samuel Whitson. March 27, 1758.

Joan Chapman Purnell dec.
William Ashmore and Francis Purnell Adm.; Thos. Harrison and John Baylis Gent. March 27, 1758.

Gilbert Crupper dec.
Elizabeth Crupper Adm.; Howson Kenner, and James Seaton. May 22, 1758.

Francis Searson dec.
George Harper Adm.; Thomson Mason. Aug. 28, 1758.

Bryant Shamlin dec.
Aaron Shamlin Adm.; Charles Hardin and John Lynn. Oct. 23, 1758.

George Dodson dec.
Margaret Dodson Adm.; Lazerous Dodson and Mackegie Pool. Nov. 27, 1758.

George Junkison dec.
William Bennitt Adm.; Isaac Davis, William Colelough. Nov. 27, 1758.

Benj. Parker dec.
William Suddorth and Rosanna Suddorth his wife Adm.; W. Ellzey. Nov. 27,

1758

Edwd. Castry dec.
Sarah Castry Adm.; Thomas Redman and Thomas Bland. March 26, 1759.

John Linton dec.
Burr Harrison Adm.; Thos. Harrison and Cuthbert Harrison. April 23, 1759.

Alexa. Ballinger dec.
James Burn Adm.; John Diskin and Wm. Seale. June 25, 1759.

Thos. Bristow dec.
Robert Scott Adm.; John Moffett. Nov. 26, 1759.

Thos. Byrne dec.
Elizabeth Byrne Adm.; Nathaneil Overall and James Head. March 24, 1760.

John Dagg dec.
Sarah Dagg Adm. with the will annexed; Foushee Tebbs and John Barker. April 28, 1760.

John Dagg dec.
Thomas Dagg Adm.; Wm. Bennett and Isaac Davis. April 28, 1760.

Robert Hedges dec.
John Hedges Adm.; Mason Bennett, Thomas
Attwell and Wm. Farrow. May 26, 1760.

Joshua Davis dec.
Isaac Davis Adm.; Henry Lee and James
Triplett. July 28, 1760.

John Dagg dec.
James Triplet and Daniel Triplet Adm.;
John Hedges, Thos. Attwell. July 28, 1760.

Rachal Jackson dec.
John Jackson Adm.; William Ellzey.
Sept. 23, 1760.

Jededia Mitchel. dec.
James Nisbett ex. of Benjamin Grayson
dec. Adm; Thomas Macken and John
Graham. Jan. 26, 1761.

Robt. Stighstead dec.
Jane Simon Adm.; Benja. Rush Jr. and
William Wilson. Feb. 23, 1761.

Alexander Bell dec.
Aaron Hawkins and Mary Hawkins his wife

Adm.; William Murphey. Feb. 23, 1761.

William Hewitt dec.
Jemima Hewitt Adm.; William Barr. March 23, 1761.

William Thorn dec.
Sarah Thorn Adm.; Henry Peyton and Edward Gwatkin. May 25, 1761.

Danl. Stewart dec.
Sarah Stewart Adm.; George Calvert Jr. May 25, 1761.

John Whitledge dec.
Elizabeth Whitledge Adm; Thomas Dagg and John Graham. Oct. 26, 1761.

Elias Wickliff dec.;
Robert Wickliff Adm.; Isaac Davis. Feb. 23, 1762.

Ewell Jones dec.
William Watkins Adm.; William Whitsides and Edward Cornwell. March 22, 1762.

William Melton dec.
Sarah Melton Adm.; William Bird, and George Reeve. May 4, 1762.

John Foley dec.
James Foley Adm.; William Ellzey. June 7, 1762.

Robt. Neavil dec.
John Baylis Adm.; William Baylis.
Aug. 6, 1762.

Nathaniel Overall dec.
Thomas Machan Adm.; John Graham.
Sept. 9, 1762.

Sarah Moss dec.
Thomas Moss Adm.; Daniel Kinchelo.
Feb. 11, 1763.

Thos. Mollahaon dec.
Ann Mollahon Adm.; George Johnston.
April 8, 1763.

Sarah Melton dec.
Richard Melton Adm.; William Carr and Thomas Bland. July 4, 1763.

Jane Shadburn dec.
Richard Adams Adm.; James Tebbs. Aug. 1, 1763.

John Waters dec.

Christian Waters Adm.; William Tackett and Wm. More. Sept. 5, 1763.

John Bland dec.
John Bland Adm.; William Carr. Nov. 7, 1763.

Richard Adams dec.
Sarah Adams Adm.; Joseph Thruman and Thomas Riddle. March 1, 1764.

Richd. Morris dec.
Ann Morris Adm.; John Thomas and Andrew Martin. July 2, 1764.

Elizabeth Reno dec.
John Orear Adm.; Wm. Whitledge. May 7, 1764.

Fran. Garner dec.
William Carr, Gent., Adm.; Wm. Tebbs. May 7, 1764.

James Norris dec.
Catherine Norris Adm.; Scarlett Maddin and George Bigby. Sept. 3, 1764.

Nathl. Smith dec.
Joseph Bowman Adm.; John Gunyon. Jan. 7, 1765.

Edward Moss dec.
John Reeves Adm.; Foushee Tebbs and William Carr. March 4, 1765.

Leonard Oden dec.
Francis Oden Adm.; William Horton. March 4, 1765.

Richd. Wright Jr. dec.
Leanna Wright Adm.; William Mow and James Wilson. March 5, 1765.

Wm. Wilkerson dec.
Sarah Wilkerson Adm.; William Melton and Eli Cleveland. July 1, 1765.

Joseph Bowman dec.
Thomson Mason and William Carr, Gent. Adm.; Foushee Tebbs and James Douglass, Gent. Aug. 6, 1765.

James Hay dec.
James Triplett Adm.; Foushee Tebbs. Oct. 7, 1765.

Francis Purncel dec.
Mason Bennett Adm.; John Hedges. May 5, 1766.

Thomas Foxworthy dec.
William Carr Adm.; William Ellzey.
June 2, 1766.

Charles Bryons dec.
Samuel Byrons Adm.; Isaac Davies & William Davies. June 3, 1766

Jeckonias Cooper dec.
Robert Brent Adm.; Cuthbert Bullitt
Oct. 6, 1766.

William Sampson dec.
Mary Sampson Adm.; James Foley. Nov. 4, 1767.

Thomas Stewart dec.
Thomas Stewart Adm.; (crossed out and written Richard Stewart); John Graham..
April 6, 1767.

Thomas Davise dec.
William Barr Adm. of the will annexed.
Henry Lee and John Murray. June 2, 1767.

Sarah Caster dec.
Isabella Caster Adm.; William Carr.
Dec. 7, 1767.

Ann Farrow dec.
William Farrow Adm.; John Brett and
Hubbard Irina? Dec. 8, 1767.

Benj. Drummond dec.
Norman Drummond Adm.; Will. Wilson
and George Bigley. Feb. 1, 1768.

John Hartshorn dec.
John Hartshorn Adm.; Alex. Henderson.
March 7, 1768.

Joshua Dooing dec.
Violetta Dooing Adm. William Carr.
March 8, 1768.

Sarah English dec.
Robert English :Adm.; John English
and Thomas Carter. April 4, 1768.

Mary Wells dec.
William Carr Adm.; William Grayson
and William Cocke. Aug. 3, 1768.

Cuthbert Harrison dec.
Cuthbert Harrison Adm.; Cuthbert
Bullitt and John MacMillion. Oct. 3,
1768.

Chas. Stanton dec.
Israel Tolson Adm.; John Murray.
Feb. 6, 1769.

John Gallehus dec.
William Tackitt Adm.; Lewis Reno Jr.
April 3, 1769.

James Crouch dec.
Jacob Crouch Adm.; William Jones and
James Jones. May 1, 1769.

William Glover dec.
Martha Glover Adm.; William Askins and
Jesse More. May 1, 1769.

Wm. Wharton dec.
Mary Wharton Adm.; George Calvert.
June 5, 1769.

John McLanachan dec.
Andrew McLanachan Adm.; Anthony Seal
Jr. and William Young. Aug. 7, 1769.

Jeremiah Jordan dec.
Wm. Cocke Adm.; Foushee Tebbs. Nov. 6,
1769.

Thomas Guin dec.
Valentine Cloninger Adm.; Thomas

Marshall. Dec. 5, 1769.

John Newman dec.
Thomas Montgomorie Adm.; Thomas Lawson.
March 5, 1770.

John Rookard dec.
Charity Rookard Adm.; Valentine Cloinger
and Will. Griffin. March 6, 1770.

Joseph Collins dec.
Sarah Collins Adm.; John Nelson. April
3, 1770.

Presley Moss dec.
George Laurie Adm.; John Riddell.
April 3, 1770.

Robert Tyler dec.
John Maddox Adm.; Isaac Davise. May 9,
1770.

Aaron Hardwitch dec.
Margaret Hardwitch Adm.; John Riddell
and Hezekiah Glasscock. May 10, 1770.

Thomas Williams dec.
John Cook Adm.; Cornelius Kincheloe and
John Murray. Nov. 5, 1770.

Chas. Jackson dec.
Jane Jackson Adm.;   James Gwatkins and
John Lynn. Feb. 4, 1771.

Geo. Skinker dec.
William Skinker Adm.;   Daniel Payne and
Anthony Seale Jr. May 6, 1771.

Isaac Davis dec.
Elizabeth Davis Adm.;   Daniel Kincheloe,
Wm. Kincheloe, and Robert Wickliff.
June 3, 1771.

E'Th. Whitledge dec.
John Whitledge Adm.;   Cuthbert Harrison.
June 3, 1771.

William Ballendine dec.
Jesse Ewell Adm.;   John Murray and John
Gunyon. June 7, 1771.

John Bryant dec.
Christian Power Adm.;   James Abell and
Humphry Calvert. Sept. 6, 1771.

George Smith dec.
John Smith Adm.;   William Martin and
William Carr. Oct 7, 1771.

Gilbert Murray dec.
John Murray Adm.; William Brent and Jesse Ewell. March 3, 1772.

John Donaldson dec.
Mary Donaldson Adm.; Wm. Davis Jr. and Gerrard Woodward. April 7, 1772.

Richard Drumond dec.
John Ship Adm.; Anthony Seal Jr. and James Cullins. Mary 4, 1772.

Jane Dunlop dec.
Evan Williams Adm.; Hugh Brent. June 2, 1772.

John Powell dec.
Thomas Chapman Adm.; Evan Williams. June 3, 1772.

John Richards dec.
Mary Richards Adm.; Alex. Rigby and James Carberry. Aug. 7, 1772.

William Barr dec.
Rebecca Barr Adm.; Redman Grigsby, and Moses Suddart. Nov 2, (no year).

Thos. Brocas dec.
Jane Brocas Adm.; John Calvert and William Calvert. Dec. 9, 1772.

Wm. Horton dec.,
Charles Chaddock Adm.; George Calvert and Thomas Masterson.. March 1, 1772.

Grace Sampson dec.
Eliz. Davis Adm.; Lewis Renoe Sr. March 3, 1773.

John Neilson dec.
William Cummingham Adm.; William Carr and John Riddell. June 9, 1773.

James Woodhouse dec.
William Carr Adm.; Cuthbert Bulliett and Thomas Martt?. July 5, 1773.

Traverse Downman dec.
Thomas Chapman and John Coppedge. Nov 2, 1773.

William Wilson dec.
Christian Power Adm.; John Gunyon and Hubard Prince. March 8, 1774.

Richd. Evans dec.
Mary Evans Adm.; Thomas Lawson. May 3,

1774.

William Askin dec.
William Askin Adm.; Thomas Homes and Lewis Reno Jr. Sept. 5, 1774.

Jabez Downman dec.
Ann Downman Adm.; Jas. Nisbet, John Hancock, John Linton and Wm. Linton. Oct. 3, 1774.

Thos. Brewer dec.
Sarah Brewer Adm.; John Linton and John Calvert. Nov. 7, 1774.

Wm. O'Bryan dec.
Mary O'Bryan Adm.; John Gunyon. Jan. 2, 1775.

Mich. Monntine? dec.
Daniel Barnett Adm.; Jacob Marshall and Foley. March 6, 1775.

Mary Pierce dec.
John Pierce Adm.; Jacob Garreen Pierce. April 3, 1775.

Henry Holtzclaw dec.
Robert Dobson Adm.; Alexander Campbell.

July 3, 1774.

John Cole dec.
Jean Cole Adm.; Rodham Blansett and William Martin. Oct. 2, 1775.

Gerard Masters dec.
Thomas Masters Adm.; Thomas Homer?, William Askins. Dec. 4, 1775.

Mary Blackburn dec.
Thomas Blackburn Adm.; Cuthbert Bullitt and Jesse Ewell. Feb. 5, 1776.

William Reno dec.
Lewis Reno Jr. Adm.; James Gwatkin. May 6, 1776.

Hezekiah Gray dec.
Mary Gray Adm.; Elijah Wood and Joseph Blanset. May 6, 1776.

Mary Ann Newman dec.
John Posey Newman Adm.; Wm. Alexander and Richd. Melton. May 6, 1776.

James Hoomes dec.
Elizabeth Hoomes and Thos. Hoomes Adm.; John Whitledge and Wm. Whitledge. Oct.

7, 1776.

Mary Evans dec.
Thomas Lawson Adm.;   Thomas Chapman.
Jan. 7, 1777.
And. Leitch dec.
Thomas Aithkin Adm.;   Foushee Tebbs and
Thos. Chapman.   June 2, 1777.

James Simms? dec.
John Leewright Jr. Adm.; John Edwards,
Aug. 4, 1777.

Dorby Gallahue dec.
Jeremiah Gallahue Adm.;   John McMillion.
Aug. 4, 1777.

Thomas Reno dec.
Katy Reno Adm. John Leewright Jr.,
Scarlett Madden. Sept. 1, 1777.

Sylvester Moss dec.;   Moses Moss Adm.;
John Hooe and James Foley. Sept. 1,
1777.

Thomas Cassady dec.: Alexander Brown
Adm.
James Triplett. Oct. 6, 1777.

John Blansett dec.
Catherine Blanset Adm.;   Rhoda Blanset
and Wm. Farrow.   Nov. 3, 1777.

John Davis dec.
William Davis Jr. Adm.; Cornelius Davis. Jan. 5, 1778.

John Sims dec.
Charles Simms Adm.; Wm. Brent and John Murray. Feb. 2, 1778.

Rhueben Calvert dec.
Sarah Calvert Adm.; Wm. Farrow and William Calvert. April 6, 1778.

Richard Jervis dec.
Redman Grigsby Adm.; Timothy Peyton and Mark Tharpe. April 6, 1778.

John Callin dec.
James Cullin Adm.; Thomas Thornton. May 4, 1778.

Christ. Curtis dec.
Chichester Curtis Adm.; Robert Warren and Henry Peyton. May 4, 1778.

Wm. Watkins dec.
Henry Watkins Adm.; Thomas Thornton. July 6, 1778.

Geo: Bigbie dec.
Catherine Bigbie Adm.; John Brett.
Aug. 3, 1778.

Thos. Dagge dec.
James Triplett Adm.; Evan Williams and
William Farrow. Sept. 7, 1778.

Thos. Smith dec.
Charles Smith Adm.; Alexander
Henderson. Sept. 7, 1778.

George Foster dec.
Margaret Foster Adm.; John Hooe, Henry
Peyton and Leonard Hart. Oct. 5, 1778.

Francis Oden dec.
Violetta Oden Adm.; Thomas Blackburn.
Nov. 2, 1778.

Rhueben Wilder dec.
James White Adm.; William Herndon.
Nov. 2, 1778.

William Popejoy dec.
Ann Popejoy Adm.; Jas. Byrn. March 1,
1779.

Geo. Farrow dec.

Milly Farrow Adm.; Lewis Reno Jr. and Jno. Leewright Jr. Mar. 9, 1779.

Thos. Davis dec.
Sarah Davis Adm; George Tebbs. April 6, 1779.

William Reno dec.
Learenoe Reno Adm.; John Cheshire and Thos. Homes. Sept. 6, 1779.

T. Aitkens dec.
John Murray Adm.; Cuthbert Bullitt and Wm. Carr. April 4, 1780.

Wm. Montgomerie dec.
George Graham Adm.; John Campbell. April 4, 1780.

Dec. name left out of bond.
Francis Floyd Adm.; Henry Peyton. May 1, 1780.

James West dec.
John Lynn Adm.; Wm. Gains and William Lynn. July 3, 1780.

Richard Sprigg dec.
Edward Sprigg Adm.; Thos. Attwell and

Wm. Farrow. March 6, 1781.

Wm. Rawling dec.
Margt. Rawlings Adm.; Evan Williams.
Aug. 6, 1781.

Geo. Madden dec.
Kesiah Madden Adm.; Wm. French and John Leewright. Feb. 4, 1782.

Wm. Bird dec.
Thomas Bird Adm.; Wm. Ellzey, Wm. Brown?, and Bernd. Hooe. May 6, 1782.

Reginald Graham dec.
George Graham Adm.; William Carr and Richard Graham. June 3, 1782

John Flattery dec.
Hugh Flattery Adm.; Richd. Graham and Daniel Carroll Brent. Aug. 5, 1782.

Jona. Stout dec.
Benj. Stout Adm.; Richard Reade. Aug. 5, 1782?.

Valentine Peyton dec.
Timothy Peyton Adm.; John McMillion.
Aug. 2, 1782.

Jas. Brown dec.

Betsy Thornbury Adm.;   John McMillion.
Nov. (can not read day), 1782.

Geo. Green Jr. dec.
Eliz'th. Green Adm.;   Ja. Ewell and
Benj. Bridges. Nov. 4, 1782.

John Burrough dec.
Mary Burrough Adm.;   Moses Jeffries and
John Hodges/Hedges. Nov. 4, 1782.

INDEX

A
Abell
  James, 18
Adams/Addams
  John, 2
  Richard, 11, 12
  Sarah, 12
Aitkens/Aitken
  T., 26
  Thomas, 23
Alexander
  Wm., 22
Anderson
  Elizabeth, 6
  John, 6
Ashmore
  William, 2, 4, 7
Askins/Askin
  William, 21, 16, 22
Attwell
  Thomas, 9
  Thos., 9, 26

B
Ballendine
  William, 18
Ballinger
  Alexa., 8
Barker
  John, 8
Barnett
  Daniel, 21
Barr
  Rebecca, 19
  William, 10, 14, 19

Batton
  Catherine, 1
  Hermon, 1
Baylis
  John, 3, 4, 7, 11
  William, 11
Belfare
  James, 4
  Sarah, 4
Bell
  Alexander, 9
Bennett/Bennitt
  Mason, 2, 9, 13
  William, 7
  Wm., 8
  Mason, 2
Bigbie/Bigby/Bigly
  Catherine, 25
  Geo., 25
Bigbie
  George, 12, 15
Bird
  Thomas, 27
  William, 10
  Wm., 27
Blackburn
  Mary, 22
  Thomas, 22, 25
Blackwell
  Joseph, 5
Bland
  John, 12
  Thomas, 6, 8, 11
Blansett
  Catherine, 23
  John, 23
  Joseph, 22
  Rhoda, 23

Blansett
  Rodham, 22
Bowman
  Joseph, 12, 13
Brent
  Daniel Carroll, 27
  Hugh, 19
  William, 19
  Wm., 24
Brett
  George, 2, 4
  John, 15, 25
Brewer
  Sarah, 21
  Thos., 21
Bridges
  Benj., 28
  Benjamin, 3
  William, 3
Bristow
  Thos., 8
Brocas
  Jane, 20
  Thos., 20
Brown
  Alexander, 23
  George, 1
  Jas., 27
Brown?
  Wm., 27
Bryant
  John, 18
Bullett/Bulliett
  Cuthbert, 15, 20, 22, 26
Burgess
  Francis, 5

Burn
  James, 8
Burrough
  John, 28
  Mary, 28
Byrne/Byron/Byrons
  Charles, 14
  Elizabeth, 8
  Jas., 25
  Samuel, 14
  Thos., 8

C
Callin
  John, 24
Calvert
  George, 3, 10, 16, 20
  George Jr., 2
  Humphry, 18
  John, 20, 21
  Rhueben, 24
  Sarah, 24
  William, 20, 24
Campbell
  Alexander, 21
  John, 26
Camper
  John, 1
Carberry
  James, 19
Carr
  John, 4
  William, 4, 5, 11, 12, 13,
    14, 15, 18, 20, 27
  Wm., 26

Carter
  Thomas, 15
Cassday
  Thomas, 23
Caster
  Isabella, 14
  Sarah, 14
Castry
  Edwd., 8
  Sarah, 8
Chaddock
  Charles, 20
  see Craddock, 20
Chambling/Champlin, see Shamlin
  Aaron, 1
  Bryan Jr., 2
  William, 1

Chapman
  Thomas, 19, 20, 23
  Thos., 23
Cheshire
  John, 26
Chinn
  Charles, 4
Churchill
  Henry, 4
Cleveland
  Eli, 13
Cloinger/Cloninger
  Valentine, 16, 17
Cocke
  William, 15
  Wm., 16
Cole
  Jean, 22
  John, 22

Colelough
  William, 7
Collins
  Joseph, 17
  Sarah, 17
Conyers
  John, 3
Cook
  John, 17
Cooper
  Henry, 3
  Jeckonias, 14
Coppedge
  John, 20
Cornwell
  Edward, 10
Craddock
  see Chaddock, 20
Crouch
  Jacob, 16
  James, 16
Crupper
  Elizabeth, 7
  Gilbert, 7
  Richard, 3, 6
  Robert, 3
Cullin/Cullins
  James, 19, 24
Cummingham
  William, 20
Curtis
  Chichester, 24
  Christ., 24
  James, 6

D

Dagg
  John, 8, 9
  Sarah, 8
  Thomas, 8, 10
  Thos., 25
Dallas
  Thomas, 4
  Vylett, 4
Davis
  Cornelius, 24
  Eliz., 20
  Elizabeth, 18
  Isaac, 7, 8, 9, 10, 14, 17, 18
  John, 24
  Joshua, 9
  Sarah, 26
  Thomas, 4, 14
  Thos., 26
  William, 6, 14
  William Jr., 24
  Wm. Jr., 19
Diskin
  John, 1, 8
Dobson
  Robert, 21
Dodson
  George, 5, 7
  Lazerous, 7
  Margaret, 7
Donaldson
  John, 19
  Mary, 19
Dooing
  Joshua, 15
  Violetta, 15
Doolittle
  Thomas, 5

Douglass
  James, 3, 13
Downman
  Ann, 21
  Jabez, 21
  Traverse, 20
Drummon/Drummond
  Aaron, 1
  Benj., 15
  Norman, 15
  Richard, 19
  Thomas, 1
Duncan
  John, 5
  Joseph, 4

Dunlop
  Jane, 19

E
Edwards
  John, 23
Ellzey
  W., 5, 7
  William, 5, 6, 9, 11, 14
  Wm., 27
English
  John, 15
  Robert, 15
  Sarah, 15
Evans
  Mary, 20, 23
  Richd., 20
Ewell
  Bertrand, 4, 5
  Ja., 28

Ewell
  Jesse, 18, 19, 22

F
Farguson
  James, 2
Farrow
  Ann, 15
  Geo., 25
  Isaac, 2
  John, 1, 2
  Milly, 26
  William, 15, 25
  Wm., 9, 23, 24, 27
Fearnsley/Fearnsly
  James, 5
  Sarah, 5
Flattery
  Hugh, 27
  John, 27
Floyd
  Francis, 26
Foley
  James, 11, 14, 23
  John, 11
  Mr., 21
Foster
  George, 25
  Margaret, 25
Foxworthy
  Thomas, 14
French
  Wm., 27
Frogg
  John, 6

G
Gains
  Wm., 26
Gallahue/Gallehus
  Ann, 2
  Darby, 4
  Dorby, 23
  Jeremiah, 23
  John, 16
  William, 2
Garner
  Fran., 12
  John, 1
  Parish, 3
Glasscock
  Hezekiah, 17
Glover
  Martha, 16
  William, 16
Goon
  William, 1
Graham
  George, 26, 27
  John, 3, 9, 10, 11, 14
  Reginald, 27
  Richard, 27
  Richd., 27
Gray
  Hezekiah, 22
  Mary, 22
Grayson
  Benjamin, 9
  William, 15
Green
  Eliz'th., 28

Green
  Geo., 28
  Thomas, 6
  William, 5
Griffin
  Will., 17
Grigsby
  Redman, 19, 24
Guin
  Thomas, 16
Gunyon
  John, 12, 18, 20, 21
Gwatkin/Gwatkins
  Edward, 10
  James, 18, 22

H
Hagard
  William, 6
Hall
  Edward, 3
  Mary, 3
Hamrick
  Elizabeth, 5
  John, 5
  Robert, 5
  Sarah, 5
Hancock
  John, 21
Hardin
  Charles, 7
Hardwitch
  Aaron, 17
  Margaret, 17
Harper
  Geroge, 7
Harrison
  Burr, 8

Harrison
  Cuthbert, 8, 15, 18
  Thos., 7, 8
Hart
  Leonard, 25
Hartshorn
  John, 15
Hawkins
  Aaron, 9
  Mary, 9
Head
  James, 1, 8
Hedges/see Hodges
  John, 9, 13, 28
  Robert, 9
Helm
  Lynaugh, 4
Henderson
  Alex., 15
  Alexander, 25
Herndon
  William, 25
Hewitt
  Jemima, 10
  William, 10
Hodges/see Hedges
  John, 28
Holtzclaw
  Henry, 21
Homer?
  Thomas, 22
Hooe
  Bernd., 27
Hooe
  John, 23, 25
Hoomes/Homes
  Elizabeth, 22

Hoomes/Homes
  James, 22
  Thomas, 21, 26
  Thos., 22
Hopper
  John, 3
Horton
  William, 13
  Wm., 20

I
Irina?/ see Prince
  Hubbard, 15

J
Jackson
  Chas., 18
  Francis, 3
  Jane, 18
  John, 9
  Rackal, 9
James
  Thomas, 6
Jay
  James, 13
Jeffries
  Moses, 28
Jervis
  Richard, 24
Johnston
  George, 11
Jones
  Ewell, 10
  James, 16
  Solomon, 4

Jones
  William, 16
  Wm., **4**
Jordan
  Jeremiah, 16
Junkison
  George, 7

K
Kelly
  John, 3
  Joseph, 5

Kenner
  Howson, 7
  Richard, 2
Kincheloe/Kinchelo
  Cornelius, 17
  Daniel, 11,18
  Wm., 18

L
Laurie
  George, 17
Lawson
  Thomas, 17, 20, 23
Lee
  Henry, 3, 9, 14
Leewright
  Jno. Jr., 26
  John, 27
  John Jr., 23
Leitch
  And., 23
Linton
  John, 8, 21
  Wm., 21

Luttrell
  Simon, 2
Lynn
  John, 7, 18, 26
  William, 26

M
Machan/Macken
  Thomas, 4, 9, 11
  Thos., 6
MacMillion, 15
Madden
  Geo., 27
  Kesiah, 27
  Scarlet, 2
  Scarlett, 12, 23
Maddox
  John, 17
Marshall
  Jacob, 21
  Margaret, 2
  Richd., 6
  Robert, 2
  Robt., 2
  Thomas, 2, 6, 17
Martin
  Andrew, 12
  William, 18, 22
Martt?
  Thomas, 20
Mason
  Thomson, 7, 13
Masters
  Gerard, 22
  Thomas, 22
Masterson
  Thomas, 20

McCaul,
  David, 5
McCrae
  Allan, 3, 4, 5
McLanachan
  Andrew, 16
  John, 16
McMillion
  John, 27, 28
Melton
  Richard, 5, 11
  Richd., 22
  Sarah, 10, 11
  William, 10, 13
Metcalf
  Dianah, 6
  John, 1, 6
Miller
  William, 5
Mitchell
  Jededia, 9
  Thos., 4
Moffett
  John, 8
Mollahon
  Ann, 11
  Thos., 11
Monntine
  Mich., 21
Montgomorie/Montgomerie
  Thomas, 17
  Wm., 26
Moore
  Jesse, 16
  Wm., 12
Morris
  Ann, 12

Morris
  Richd., 12
Moss
  Edward, 13
  Moses, 23
  Presley, 17
  Sarah, 11
  Sylvester, 23
  Thomas, 11
Mow
  William, 13
Murphey
  William, 10
Murray
  Gilbert, 19
  John, 14, 16, 17, 18, 19, 24, 26

N
Neavil
  Robt., 11
Neilson
  John, 20
Nelson
  John, 17
Newman
  John, 17
  John P., 22
  Mary Ann, 22
Nisbett
  James, 9
  Jas., 21
Norris
  Catherine, 12
  James, 12

O'Bryan
  Mary, 21
  Wm., 21
Oakley
  Jemima, 3
  William, 3
Oden
  Francis, 13, 25
  Leonard, 13
  Violetta, 25
Orear
  John, 12
Overall/Overhall
  Nath., 2
  Nathaniel, 8, 11
Owen
  Francis, 6

P
Parker
  Benj., 7
Payne
  Daniel, 18
Peyton
  Henry, 10, 24, 25, 26
  John, 4
  John Jr., 2
  Timothy, 24, 27
  Valentine, 27
Pierce
  Jacob G., 21
  John, 21
Pierce
  Mary, 21
Pool
  Mackgie, 7
Pope
  Humphry, 4

Popejoy
  Ann, 25
  William, 25
Poulson
  Henry, 1
Powell
  John, 19
Power
  Christian, 18, 20
Prince
  Hubard, 20
Purncell/Purcell/Purnell
  Francis, 7, 13
  Joan Chapman, 7
  John, 2

R
Raimey
  Absolom, 5
Rawling
  Margt., 27
  Wm., 27
Reade
  Richard, 27
Redman
  Thomas, 8
Reeves/Reeves
  George, 10
  John, 13
Reno/Renoe
  Elizabeth, 12
  Katy, 23
  Learenoe, 26
  Lewis Jr., 16, 21, 22, 26
  Lewis Sr., 20
  Thomas, 23
  William, 22, 26

Richards
  John, 19
  Mary, 19
Riddell/Riddle
  John, 17, 20
  Thomas, 12
Rigby
  Alex., 19
Rizey
  Richard, 6
Rookard
  Charity, 17
Rookard
  John, 17
  William, 1, 2
Rush
  Benja. Jr., 9
Russell
  Wm., 3

S
Sampson
  Grace, 20
  Mary, 14
  William, 14
Scott
  Mary, 3
  Robert, 8
  Thos., 3
Seale/Seele/Seales
  Anthony Jr., 16, 18, 19
  Waller, 3
  Wm., 8
Searson
  Francis, 7
Seaton
  James, 7

Settle
  Martin, 1
  Mary, 1
  Strother, 1
Shadburn
  Jane, 11
Shamlin, see Champlin
  Aaron, 7
  Bryant, 7
Ship
  John, 19
Sias
  John, 4
Simmons
  John, 2
Simms/Sims
  Charles, 24
  James, 23
  John, 24
Simon
  Jane, 9
Sinclair
  Robert, 6
Skinker
  Geo., 18
  William, 18
Smith
  Charles, 25
  George, 6, 18
  Jacob, 1
  John, 6, 18
  Nathl., 12
  Thos., 25
Spillger
  William, 5
Sprigg
  Edward, 26

Sprigg
  Richard, 26
Stamps
  Ledia, 4
  Thomas, 4
Stanton
  Chas., 16
Steale/Steele
  Mathew, 3, 4, 6
Stewart
  Danl., 10
  Richard, 14
  Sarah, 10
  Thomas, 14
Stighstead
  Robt., 9
Stone
  Samuel, 5
  Thomas, 5
Stout
  Benj., 27
  Jona., 27
Suddart/Suddorth
  Moses, 19
  Rosanna, 7
  William, 7
Summers
  Elizabeth, 1
  John, 1

T
Tackett
  William, 5, 12, 16
Tebbs
  Foushee, 3, 8, 13, 16, 23
  George, 26
  James, 11
  Wm., 12

Tharpe
  Mark, 24
Thomas
  John, 12
Thorn
  Sarah, 10
  William, 1, 10
Thornbury
  Betsy, 28
Thornton
  Thomas, 24
Thruman
  Joseph, 12
Tolson
  Israel, 16
Towers
  James, 3
Triplett
  Daniel, 9
  James, 9, 13, 23, 25
Tyler
  John, 6
  Robert, 17

W
Ward
  Thos., 1
Warren
  Robert, 24
Waters
  Christian, 12
  John, 11
Watkins
  Anne, 2
  Henry, 2, 24
  William, 2, 10
  Wm., 24

Wells
  Mary, 15
West
  James, 26
Wharton
  Mary, 16
  Wm., 16
White
  James, 25
Whitesides
  William, 10
Whitledge
  E'th., 18
  Elizabeth, 10
  John, 10, 18, 22
  Wm., 12, 22
Whitson
  Samuel, 7
Wickliff
  Elias, 10
  Robert, 10, 18
Wilder
  Rhueben, 25
Wilkerson
  Sarah, 13
  Wm., 13
Williams
  Evan, 19, 25, 27
  Thomas, 17
  Thos., 1
Wilson
  James, 13
  Jean, 6
  John, 6
  Will., 15
  William, 9, 20

Wood
  Elijah, 22
Woodhouse
  James, 20
Woodward
  Gerrard, 19
Wright
  John, 3
  Leanna, 13
  Richd. Jr., 13

Y
Young
  James, 4
  William, 16

www.ingramcontent.com/pod-product-compliance
Lightning Source LLC
Chambersburg PA
CBHW071759040426
42446CB00012B/2632